MAY   2017

Peas and Cheese

Pam Scheunemann

Consulting Editor, Diane Craig, M.A./Reading Specialist

ABDO
Publishing Company

Published by ABDO Publishing Company, 4940 Viking Drive, Edina, Minnesota 55435.

Printed in the United States.

Credits
Edited by: Pam Price
Curriculum Coordinator: Nancy Tuminelly
Cover and Interior Design and Production: Mighty Media
Photo and Illustration Credits: BananaStock Ltd., Comstock, Corbis Images, Digital Vision, Francis Hammond/PhotoAlto, Hemera, Tracy Kompelien, PhotoDisc, Stockbyte, Thinkstock

Library of Congress Cataloging-in-Publication Data

Scheunemann, Pam, 1955-
     Peas and cheese / Pam Scheunemann.
       p. cm. -- (Rhyme time)
     ISBN 1-59197-810-6 (hardcover)
     ISBN 1-59197-916-1 (paperback)
     1. English language--Rhyme--Juvenile literature. I. Title. II. Rhyme time (ABDO Publishing Company)

PE1517.S44 2004
428.1'3--dc22
                                                                              2004050795

SandCastle™ books are created by a professional team of educators, reading specialists, and content developers around five essential components that include phonemic awareness, phonics, vocabulary, text comprehension, and fluency. All books are written, reviewed, and leveled for guided reading, early intervention reading, and Accelerated Reader® programs and designed for use in shared, guided, and independent reading and writing activities to support a balanced approach to literacy instruction.

Let Us Know

After reading the book, SandCastle would like you to tell us your stories about reading. What is your favorite page? Was there something hard that you needed help with? Share the ups and downs of learning to read. We want to hear from you! To get posted on the ABDO Publishing Company Web site, send us e-mail at:

sandcastle@abdopub.com

SandCastle Level: Fluent

Words that rhyme do
not have to be spelled the
same. These words rhyme
with each other:

bees

peas

cheese

please

ease

sees

freeze

tease

keys

trees

Cody is good at math.

He solves the problem on the board with **ease**.

The white-fronted bee-eater lives in Africa and eats bees.

Alexa and her mom bundle up so they won't **freeze**.

Blake and Jackie help make dinner.

They grate the **cheese**.

Bailey and Melanie are eating chicken with french fries and **peas**.

Debbie is typing on the computer **keys** with one hand.

When Leah wants her dad to give her a piggyback ride, she says **please**.

For his experiment, Nicholas looks through the microscope and records what he **sees**.

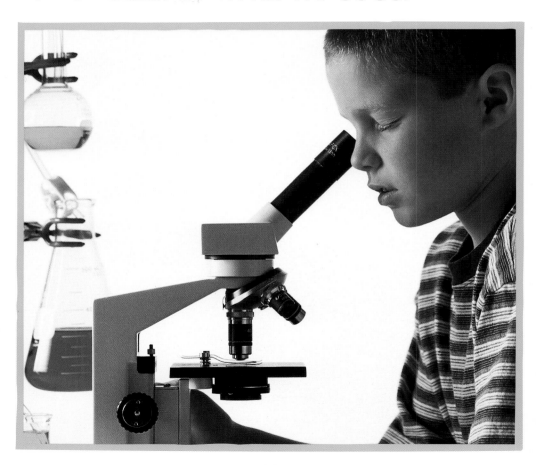

Ray sticks his tongue out at Haley because he likes to **tease**.

Andrew likes to climb trees.

Peas and Cheese

Behind our house,
up in the trees,
there lived a gang
of hungry bees.

Their favorite foods were peas and cheese.

When they wanted more, they didn't say please.

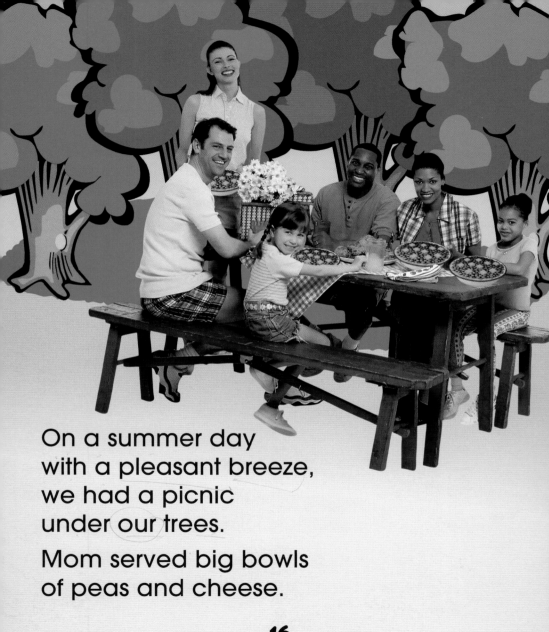

On a summer day
with a pleasant breeze,
we had a picnic
under our trees.

Mom served big bowls
of peas and cheese.

The hungry bees spied a prize
that they could seize with ease.

They put on black masks
and left the trees.

Dad cried out,
"Oh no, Louise!

The bees are coming
in twos and threes!"

The bees swarmed down
and shouted, "Freeze!
Give us all your
peas and cheese!"

Mom then said,
"We shouldn't tease
these robber bees.

Let them have
our peas and cheese."

Our peas and cheese
sure did appease
that gang of
hungry robber bees.

Rhyming Riddle

What do you call
oaks that grow cheddar?

Cheese trees

Glossary

appease. to do something to calm or satisfy others

ease. easily and effortlessly

gang. a group of people who have the same goals or interests

grate. to shred by rubbing on something rough or sharp

microscope. a magnifying device used to look at things that are too small for the eye to see

seize. to grab or take something

tease. to annoy or make fun of another person

About SandCastle™

A professional team of educators, reading specialists, and content developers created the SandCastle™ series to support young readers as they develop reading skills and strategies and increase their general knowledge. The SandCastle™ series has four levels that correspond to early literacy development in young children. The levels are provided to help teachers and parents select the appropriate books for young readers.

Emerging Readers
(no flags)

Beginning Readers
(1 flag)

Transitional Readers
(2 flags)

Fluent Readers
(3 flags)

These levels are meant only as a guide. All levels are subject to change.

ABDO
Publishing Company

To see a complete list of SandCastle™ books and other nonfiction titles from ABDO Publishing Company, visit www.abdopub.com or contact us at:
4940 Viking Drive, Edina, Minnesota 55435 • 1-800-800-1312 • fax: 1-952-831-1632